A Mess

Kristine Duran

BookLeaf Publishing

Presentation by *BookLeaf Publishing*

Web: www.bookleafpub.com

E-mail: info@bookleafpub.com

ISBN: 9789357211109

First edition 2022

DEDICATION

To myself:

Keep writing it all down.

Adulthood

Happiness doesn’t last.
At least,
Not for me.
Sadness seeps into
my skin,
pools inside my veins,
and nothing can
drain that feeling away,
ever.

Isn’t it funny?

How when you first meet
(A potential lover)
You tend to hide all
The parts of you
That would send
Any smart person
running?
Both of you
Calm
And collected
Until the
Relationship
Settles
And the ugly
Habits
Take hold
Showing
Just how
Annoying
This person
Really is.

Fucking
All night
Turns to

Silence
After fights
With both
Parties
Broken.

Porcupine shards
Of glass protecting
What's left
As you both
Move on
To the next.
Not realizing
Those quills
From the past
are stabbing
Others.

We continue to hurt
Because we've been hurt.

Crush

I search for you constantly but you're never
there.

You pace through my mind without being aware.

You're consuming my life and you don't even
care.

I am nothing to you and it's really not fair.

Nymph

She was still beautiful. It was a different kind of beauty though. What was once an ethereal loveliness, something similar to that of a fairy or a nymph in a forest, turned into a hauntingly, sad type of elegance. It almost hurt to look at her but I could not pry my eyes away. She was disappearing within herself, fading and fading away until there would be nothing left. No trace of her existence at all. And I wanted nothing more than to hold her close. Hold her tight to my chest until her color came back, until she blossomed into that strong flower that once danced in the sunlight of others affection. But she was drooping and her petals were wafting to the ground.

Anxiety

The day was winding down
so were we
I had stopped crying.
My heaves diminished
back to natural breaths.

Your body,
a mountain before me,
vast and scarred
each valley a story
I've heard too many times.

I'm looking into you
and see nothing
You are doing the same
It is quiet
not even the birds
will disturb
this moment.

I don't dare
open my mouth
for fear
it will start up again

not after
its taken this long
to calm me.

If my mind were anything,
it would be a hurricane.
My body: the eye of the storm,
the deceitful core
that will not
give up
this peaceful facade.

Your fingers,
the only movement
back and forth
where my hairline
meets my forehead,
Keeping the anxiety away.

Home Sweet Home

I built my home out of a person,
all vulnerable flesh, tendon and bone.
I built my home out of a person,
instead of constructing it on its own.

I could not have chosen a riskier feat
by investing it on a single soul.
When it all began to turn to shit,
i found that i was no longer whole.

I built my home out of a person,
a sounder decision by me could not be felt.
I built my home out of a person,
but I set fire to it myself.

Hypocrite

When I see my scars
it's like reminiscing on past love affairs.
Each one gave me
what I needed at the time.
A certain pleasure
fills me
when I graze them
with my fingertips.
I can recall
The rush
Of adrenaline
From each
Raised line.

When I see scars on her
my heart stops.
It becomes hard
to breathe as I picture her
dragging blades
against skin.
I want to see past them
I wish I could ignore them.
But all I see are those scars,
all I feel is what
she must have felt
to make them in the first place.

Flashbacks

My knees feel like they might buckle,
my heartbeat suddenly weak.
If I had any thoughts to express,
I would not be able to speak.

It comes out of nowhere,
at the most inconvenient moment.
Being alone with my thoughts have
become the very worst torment.

I just can't seem to control it,
the numbness constantly ripples through.
Everything seems to slip away
whenever my mind brings up memories of you.

Boyfriend

I wanted to run out naked
so that everyone would see
and know what had happened.
It's 2 AM and everyone is asleep.

How could they not hear my screams?
Even before being muffled by your hands

I thought seriously about calling the cops
but realized that it would do no good.

It didn't matter
that I was crying
and scared
because apparently
it's not rape
if he's your boyfriend.

Not when he'll say
"She always wants it anyways."
"She has all these fantasies."
"This is just how she is."

Hello My Name Is Baby

There was a time when you would
call me your girl with such pride.
I never thought the sound of you
saying my name would hurt me this much.

Fantasies

I can picture it.
4 bottles of extra strength aspirin, value size.
5 bottles of vodka to chase.
The letter arriving at your house.
Would you punch the wall in rage
Knowing that you caused it?

That's so fucked up.
I know, I know, I'm so fucked up.

Desperate Times

It took me 27 steps to get to my car that night. 27 steps instead of throwing a brick into your window. 27 painful steps knowing that nothing would be the same once I drove off. 27 fucking steps instead of slashing my throat and bleeding out on your porch. 27 steps instead of crawling on hands and knees, begging you to keep me.

All I Can Think About Is…

You.
Smoking your brand
of cigarettes
and how
the wisps of smoke
mingle
with each strand
of your hair
how the smell of it
lingers there
for me
to experience
at night when my face
caresses yours.

Fairytale

You told me I was the type of girl
who had a chip on her shoulder.
It was preposterous then.
Three years later,
I'm realizing that maybe..
just maybe,
you were right.

Because who really
wants to admit
something like that?

~

Yes dear, I'm selfish.
Yes, I deserve the world.
I refuse to settle.

Is this really how this goes?
Shouldn't he give me
the world if I ask for it?
If he's the one
shouldn't he make me feel like the only one?

Told You So

But it was you who left me
when you said you wouldn’t
when I said you would

It was you who left me
when you said I was home
and I said I'm no good

It was you who left me
when you said you'd always love me
and I didn't see how you could

Liar

You are not
A man of
Your word
If you
Pick and
Choose
Which
Words to
Keep.

Loser

I never fought for anything
as hard as I fought for you
and I still lost.

Midnight Musings

How could you do that to me?
How could you do that to me?
How could you do that to me?
How could you do that to me?
How could you do that to me?
How could you do that to me?
How could you do that to me?
How could you do that to me?
How could you do that to me?
How could you do that to me?
How could you do that to me?
How could you do that to me?
How could you do that to me?
How could you do that to me?
How could you do that to me?
How could you do that to me?
How could you do that to me?
How could you do that to me?

Stress Eating

You know that feeling when you've had a day
and you think to yourself, I really need some
comfort food.
Well, you're my favorite bowl of chili with a
side of cornbread.
You're that sweet drizzle of honey and butter that
I certainly do not need, but will eat anyways.

www.ingramcontent.com/pod-product-compliance
Lightning Source LLC
Chambersburg PA
CBHW051720130826
49812CB00034B/1280